Stop!

Don't Touch My Danger Zone! Activity Book

Written by AW Leak
Curtis L. Speed, MD, Consultant

Published by Courageous Kids, Inc. P.O. Box 2322, CCH, IL 60478
Order on line at ShopCKids.com

ISBN: 978-0-9742590-2-4

Library of Congress Registration Number Txu-348-303

Author: AW Leak
AKA Auntie Wina

Cover Design/Layout Cecil Anderson
William Morris, Illustrator p.14, 15

Address all inquiries to
Courageous Kids, Inc.
P.O. Box 2322
Country Club Hills, IL 60478

Printed in the United States of America

Order on line at www.CreateACourageousKid.com
or E-mail at BeCourageous@cs.com
1-708-922-9233

The Author does not represent herself as a physician or psychologist and the recommendations in this book are not intended to replace advice from health care professionals. It is intended to be used as preventive measures and an additional resource for parents, educators and those who work with children. Those with physical, mental or emotional health issues should seek advice from their health care provider.

Dedication

Dear God,

Thank You for:

Your unconditional Love.

My healing.

Using me as an instrument of Peace.

Divine Order.

All of the Foot Soldiers who you sent to help me to this point and even carried me when I thought I could go no further.

The millions of children who will read these words and protect themselves from hurt, harm and danger.

Your Humble Servant,

AW Leak aka Auntie Wina

Dear Parent,

Welcome to my third children's book, Stop! Don't Touch My Danger Zone! Activity Book. According to the National Sexual Violence Resource Center (NSVRC) the statistics are one (1) out of every (3) girls and (1) in every (6) boys will be sexually assaulted by the age of 18*. For most children, it is a matter of when, not if.

We cannot be around our children 24 hours a day. An effective technique is needed to protect them from the growing number of sexual predators when they are away from our watchful eyes. The perpetrators are smart, therefore we must outsmart them using education as our weapon.

Criminals work in the dark and fear exposure. So many children are victimized in places where help is just steps away or in an adjacent room. Therefore, it is imperative that we first, teach our children which parts of the body are "off limits" to others. Secondly, we must ingrain an effective response if/when they find themselves in this situation.

These series of child safety books, Stop! Don't Touch My Danger Zone! Activity Book and Who Is Stranger Danger?! are designed to facilitate an ongoing conversation between you and your child. Children learn by repetition. This book uses the analogy of traffic signs and warning sounds to create imagery for your child. Therefore, each time you drive with your child and stop at a stop light, this could be an opportunity for a memorable safety conversation that your child will recall when you are not around.

Should your child disclose he or she has been inappropriately touched, believe them. Most children do not lie about this topic. If you suspect something has happened, view our website, www.CreateACourageousKid.com for Signs of Abuse. Please do not make them a victim for the second time by responding negatively or in disbelief but give them the support they will so desperately need from you.

Many who are molested, molest others. By changing this vicious cycle, our children will grow up and go to college instead of going to jail and leading dysfunctional lives.

I use the name Auntie Wina because I am trying to be an Aunt to all children and I challenge each one of you to do the same. With your help, we can change the world.

Blessings,
AW Leak aka Auntie Wina
Founder, Courageous Kids, Inc.

*Finkelhor, David, et.al. "Sexual Abuse in a National Survey of Adult Men and Women: Prevalence, Characteristics and Risk Factors," Child Abuse and Neglect, 1990

Secrets

Do you know what a secret is?

Can you spell the word, "Secret"? Write it on the line below.

secrets

There are good secrets and bad secrets.

A good secret is knowing your best friend is going to have a surprise birthday party. You don't want to tell her because it will spoil the surprise!

It's ok not to tell a good secret.

Color the picture above.

Good Secret

A good secret is saving lots of money in your Courageous Kid's Lion Bank. Only you know how much treasure is in the Courageous Lion's tummy!

Hey! Maybe you have enough money to buy your best friend a gift for her surprise birthday party!

Color the Courageous Kid's Lion Bank yellow.

What is a bad secret?

A bad secret is something that you have seen, heard, done or has happened to you. This secret makes you feel bad and you believe you can't tell anyone.

If someone touches your body in a certain place or places, you may feel bad or want to cry. Then, this person tells you not to tell anyone.

This is a bad secret.

If you tell the right person your bad secret, they can help you feel better. Tell your parent or teacher one good secret and one bad secret.

If you had a secret, good or bad, who would you tell?

Could this person help you with your secret? If one person cannot help, tell someone else.

Let's name the people you can tell! Write the names of 5 people, who can help like your parents, your teachers, your grandma or grandpa, aunts, uncles or principal.

Ask your parent or teacher to help you write your list!

MOM

Dad

Teacher

Friend

Feelings

We have good feelings and bad feelings.

Draw a line to the word that best describes how you feel when you look at the picture.

Good

Bad

Fear

Courage

Good feelings make us laugh, smile, jump and play.

We like to feel good.

Why are the boy and girl smiling?

Color the picture with your favorite colors.

Bad feelings make us cry, frown and look sad.

Why is this boy feeling sad?

Fear is a bad feeling.

Fear is a feeling you have if you believe someone or something will hurt you.

Why is this little boy afraid?

Color the picture.

Courage

Did you know you can choose the way you feel?

This little girl could have chosen to feel **courage**, not fear.

The examination did not hurt like she believed it would!

When you visit your doctor, be **courageous**!

Do you want to be a Courageous Kid?

Feeling courageous makes you strong like a lion!

You are not afraid.

Be brave! Be Courageous!

Colors

It is fun to ride in a car and look out of the windows!

On many street corners, there are many stop lights that look like tall green or black poles with rectangle shapes at the top.

Did you see a stop light when you traveled to school today?

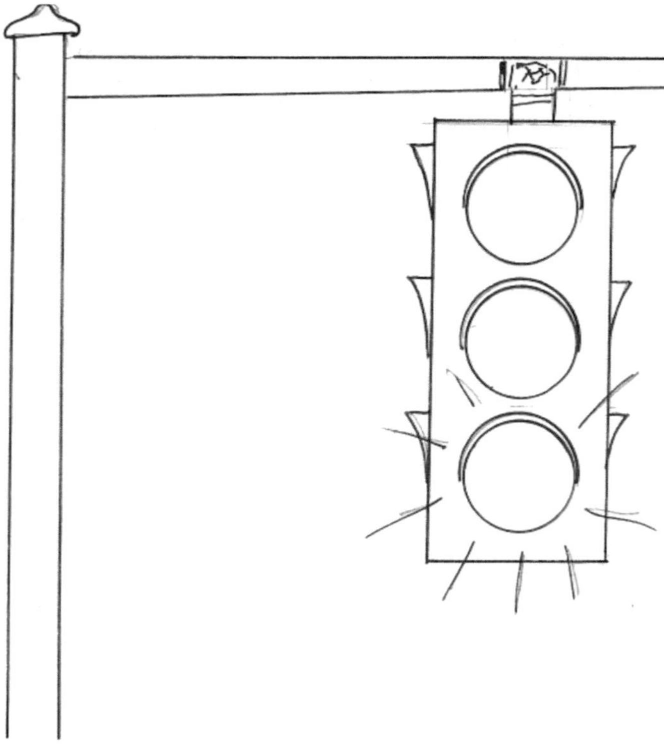

In the rectangle, count each circle.

Color the circle at the top red.

Color the circle in the middle yellow.

Color the circle on the bottom green.

Green Means Go!

If the stop light is green, it is ok to GO!

Yellow

The next time you see a stoplight, watch it turn colors!

When the green light goes off, the yellow light in the middle turns on. This yellow light is a symbol telling us "Warning"! Sometimes this yellow circle will flash.

A "Warning" sign means something bad can happen if things continue. A yellow light, a yellow flashing light or a diamond shaped yellow sign means, "Slow down! Be Careful!"

A yellow circle on the stoplight tells the driver, "Slow down, get ready to stop!" If the driver does not slow down or stop, a car accident could happen. Someone can get hurt, feel pain or feel bad.

Color the middle circle in the stoplight yellow!

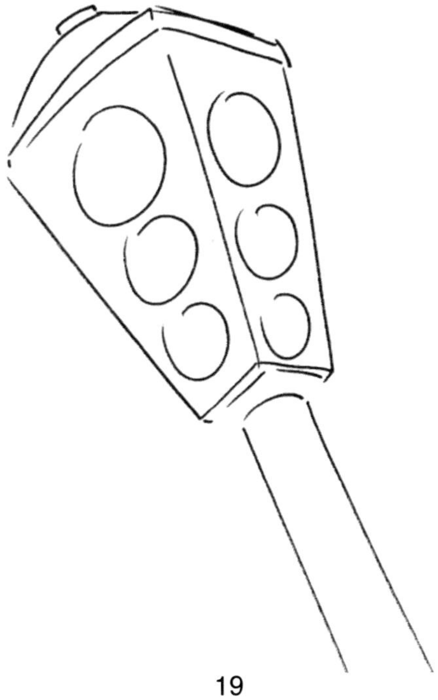

A "Warning" sign means something bad can happen if things continue.

A yellow light, a yellow flashing light or a diamond shaped yellow sign means, "Slow down! Be Careful!"

Color the diamond shaped Warning sign yellow.

Warning Sounds

Listen! The train is coming! Can you hear the clanging bell or the loud horn? The train is warning the cars and people to stop!

A police car speeding fast through the streets will flash spinning blue lights. The siren screams loudly in the air as the car whizzes by!

Can you make a warning sound like the police siren?

Red

Red is the color in the top circle of the stoplight. Red means, "Stop! Don't go any further! Don't move! Be still! Stop! Danger is near!"

A red circle tells the driver in your car or bus not to move because it is not safe to proceed.

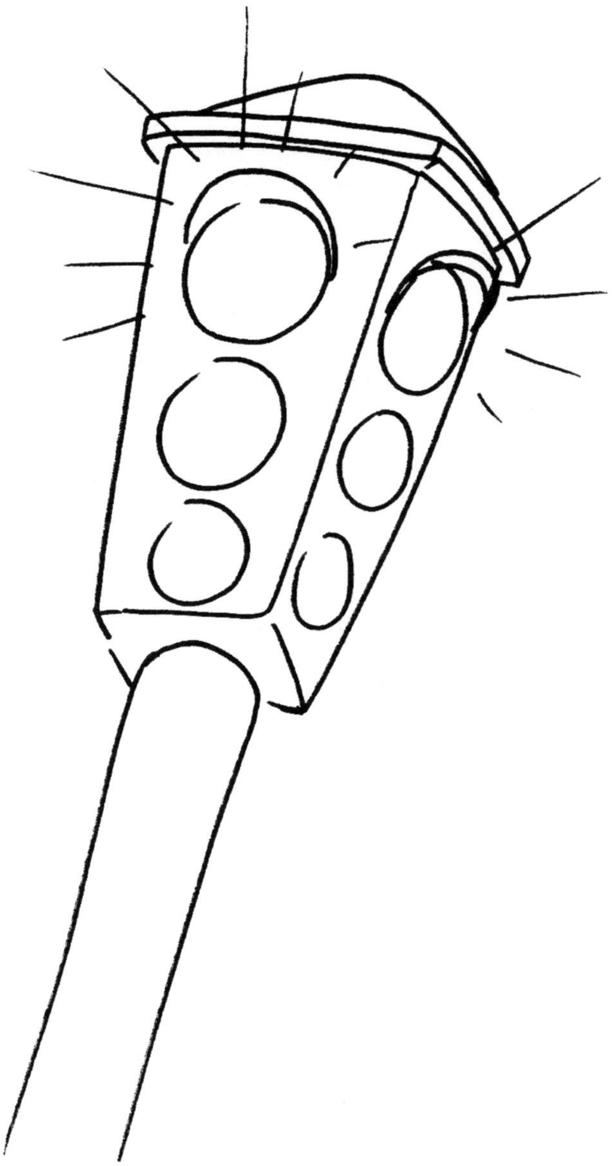

Color the top circle in the stoplight red!

Write the word Danger on the line above.

Someone or something that brings danger or is dangerous can hurt you or make you feel bad.

Have you ever seen a red octagon sign with the word STOP written in white letters?

This sign tells your parents to STOP the car! Do not move ahead until it is save to drive!

Count each side of the Stop sign.

The red, eight sided STOP sign looks like this.

Can you draw a red Stop sign, too? Does your sign have 8 sides?

Count the sides with your parent or teacher. If your sign has eight sides, you have created an octagon!

Our Bodies

Draw your body here.

Don't forget to use your favorite colors!

Let's call each part of your body a "Zone".

A zone is a place that has a special purpose.

Write the word Zone on the line below.

A

Zone A is your pretty head! You use it to think, talk, see, hear, listen, smell, breath, sing and smile.

What else can you do with your head?

Color the friendly faces!

Draw your pretty face on this page!

Strong arms and hands are found in Zone B.

B

Your flexible hands can write, wave and color.

The big muscles in your arms help you to do push-ups and carry your books.

Strike a pose! Show the strong muscles in your arms and hands like the boy and girl.

You are beautiful!

Draw your arms and hands. Now color them!

C

Running legs and walking feet
are in Zone C.

Name other activities you can do with your legs and feet.

Draw your legs and feet! Have fun coloring them!

The Danger Zone

D

Zone D is the **Danger Zone**! The Danger Zone is any area on the boys and girls where the Stop signs are.

If anyone tries to touch your body in the Danger Zones, they could be Stranger Danger.

We call Zone D, " The Danger Zone" to help you tell others if you need help from Stranger Danger.

Your body is special and made just for you and only you! From the tip of your head to your tiniest toe, your body is a miraculous work of art. The parts of your body underneath the Stop signs are little miracles, too!

Ask your parent or teacher to name the body parts underneath the Stop signs.

A Stop sign means danger could be near.

Someone touching your body in the Danger Zone areas could be Stranger Danger.

Big, small, thick or tall, YOU OWN YOUR BODY! You are in charge of this magnificent work of art!

Even if someone is bigger than you, do not be afraid to say, "Stop! Don't Touch My Danger Zone!" as loud as you can.

Look at the Warning signs on the boy and girl.

If someone touches you in the yellow Warning Zone and then moves to the Red Danger Zone, scream "Stop! Don't Touch My Danger Zone!"

Color the Warning signs yellow and the Stop signs red.

Stranger Danger has many faces. Boy or girl, man or woman may want to touch you in the Danger Zone.

You have the right to say "No" because you are in charge of your body. It belongs to You!

Extend your hand like the Crossing guard.

This officer stops the cars so you can cross the street safely.

Practice with your parents or teachers. Say, "Stop! Don't Touch My Danger Zone! " as loud as you can.

If a boy or girl, man or woman wants you to touch their Danger Zone, scream "NO! I WILL NOT TOUCH YOUR DANGER ZONE!"

This is not a bad secret. Have **courage!** **Do not be afraid.**

Tell your Mom, Dad or teacher what happened. They will want to know.

Now say, "No!" as loud as you can.

No! No!

No! No!

No! No!

Practice with your parent or teacher. Use your loudest voice!

Your parents and teachers love you. You can tell them any secret, bad or good, and they will still love you!

The Courageous Kid Pledge

I may be small
But inside, I am tall.
This body, I own.
And You Can't Touch My
Danger Zone!

Glossary

Courage

"A strength that a person has that helps him or her to face danger by overcoming fear; bravery."[1]

Danger

"1. A chance that something bad or harmful will happen. 2. Something that may cause harm or injury."[2]

Fear

"A strong feeling caused by knowing that danger, pain, or evil is near."[3]

Mask
"1. A covering worn to hide or protect the face...2. Anything that hides or covers up something."[4]

Octagon

"A figure having eight sides and eight angles."[5]

Stranger

"A person whom one does not know."[6]

Warn

"1. To put on guard by giving notice beforehand; caution."[7]

Zone

2. Any region or area that has some special quality, condition or use."[8]

Footnotes

1. William D. Halsey,Editorial Director, Christopher G. Morris, Editor, P. R. Winant, Supervising Editor, Vesta K. Wells;Natalie Hilzen; Katherine A. Brodie; Robert K. Haycraft; Nacy B. Nightingale; Pamaela M Nugent; Deborah DiGiovanna, Macmillan Dictionary For Children, Revised Edition, p. 150.
2. William D. Halsey,Editorial Director, Christopher G. Morris, Editor, P. R. Winant, Supervising Editor, Vesta K. Wells;Natalie Hilzen; Katherine A. Brodie; Robert K. Haycraft; Nacy B. Nightingale; Pamaela M Nugent; Deborah DiGiovanna, Macmillan Dictionary For Children, Revised Edition, p. 166-167.
3. William D. Halsey,Editorial Director, Christopher G. Morris, Editor, P. R. Winant, Supervising Editor, Vesta K. Wells;Natalie Hilzen; Katherine A. Brodie; Robert K. Haycraft; Nacy B. Nightingale; Pamaela M Nugent; Deborah DiGiovanna, Macmillan Dictionary For Children, Revised Edition, p. 236.
4. William D. Halsey,Editorial Director, Christopher G. Morris, Editor, P. R. Winant, Supervising Editor, Vesta K. Wells;Natalie Hilzen; Katherine A. Brodie; Robert K. Haycraft; Nacy B. Nightingale; Pamaela M Nugent; Deborah DiGiovanna, Macmillan Dictionary For Children, Revised Edition, p.389.

1. William D. Halsey,Editorial Director, Christopher G. Morris, Editor, P. R. Winant, Supervising Editor, Vesta K. Wells;Natalie Hilzen; Katherine A. Brodie; Robert K. Haycraft; Nacy B. Nightingale; Pamaela M Nugent; Deborah DiGiovanna, Macmillan Dictionary For Children, Revised Edition, p. 433.
2. William D. Halsey,Editorial Director, Christopher G. Morris, Editor, P. R. Winant, Supervising Editor, Vesta K. Wells;Natalie Hilzen; Katherine A. Brodie; Robert K. Haycraft; Nacy B. Nightingale; Pamaela M Nugent; Deborah DiGiovanna, Macmillan Dictionary For Children, Revised Edition, p. 620.
3. William D. Halsey,Editorial Director, Christopher G. Morris, Editor, P. R. Winant, Supervising Editor, Vesta K. Wells;Natalie Hilzen; Katherine A. Brodie; Robert K. Haycraft; Nacy B. Nightingale; Pamaela M Nugent; Deborah DiGiovanna, Macmillan Dictionary For Children, Revised Edition, p. 697.
4. William D. Halsey,Editorial Director, Christopher G. Morris, Editor, P. R. Winant, Supervising Editor, Vesta K. Wells;Natalie Hilzen; Katherine A. Brodie; Robert K. Haycraft; Nacy B. Nightingale; Pamaela M Nugent; Deborah DiGiovanna, Macmillan Dictionary For Children, Revised Edition, p. 724.